BU

WRITE TO WIN.
Business English & Professional Email Writing Essentials: How to Write Emails for Work

BUSINESS ENGLISH ORIGINALS ©

INCLUDING 100 + BUSINESS EMAIL TEMPLATES

Topics Covered in this business English book:

Professional email, email writing, business letters, how to write a letter, how to write emails, business email, how to write business letters, Business English, business English writing, business writing, ESL business English, business English grammar, better business writing, business letters, writing business letters, business email book, writing business emails, business email writing.

Contents

"Emailing is like sex: everyone thinks they're good at it"

Author Unknown

About this Professional Email Book

Professional emails are too important to mess up. They are evidence of something that you said or did, and as such, they can be your best friend or your worst nightmare.

Every day a staggering amount of business communication takes place. This book will help you not only write more professional business e-mails but also improve your overall business English.

"Know your context as well as your audience."

Like everything in life, emails are not created equal. The same email can be digital gold or digital poop depending on the situation in which it's deployed, so you must always pay attention to context. Even if you send exactly the same email to the same audience, in a different context they will interpret your email differently, as they will approach it with a different mind-frame, together with a different set of beliefs and expectations.

When you approach an email in a business setting, the first thing to do is to decide exactly what you want from the exchange and then, what context you are writing in. Is this a close colleague but there is a not-so-close colleague included into the email exchange? Is this an invitation to have drinks after work with someone who has worked with you for years and has suddenly decided to change paths in their career? Are you about to fire someone you respect immensely? Are you sending a group email to organise a meeting, or are you asking someone to pay you because they haven't paid their invoice on time again? All these things matter, and are particularly important because you don't have the benefit of body language or facial expressions when you write. People also tend to forget verbal exchanges more readily, but the written word is powerful.

"The pen is "mightier than the sword..." (Edward Bulwer-Lytton) and people will judge you based on how you use your pen.

Contributors & Influencers

I could not possibly list all the people who have influenced me through their work, but I will try to mention a few of the ones who spring to mind in no particular order. These are my business heroes, and without their contribution through their work, I would never have been able to write this book.

If you have never read their books, and are interested in business and entrepreneurship, I implore you to go out, and buy them and read them over, and over again.

Gary Vaynerchuk

Pat Flynn

Dan Meredith

Timothy Ferriss

Dale Carnegie

Danny Rubin

Hassan Osman

Megan Sharma

William Strunk Jr.

The 16 Rules of Professional Business Email Writing for 25-year Old me

If I could write a note of advice about emails and business communication to the 25-year old Marc, I would probably send him the following checklist. I wish someone had told me all this.

1. Forget your ego. Never write with the objective of impressing someone, even if that someone is you! Sometimes we write and then re-read what we have written a few times, then we give ourselves a mental round of applause before sending it. The problem is, our priority wasn't communication in this scenario, it was to feed our ego. Trying to impress people with long over-complicated sentences and words has the opposite effect. Always keep clear communication and context in mind in every exchange.

2. Aim to explain difficult concepts or problems in a simple easy-to-understand way. This shows intelligence, because it means you have digested the concepts and are skilful enough to explain them. When you make concepts sound more complicated than they are, it gives people the impression that you don't understand, because you probably don´t.

3. If it's not relevant to the situation or the decision being made, don't mention it, it will clutter your communication and could cause confusion.

4. When you need to write important or sensitive emails, stick to the facts. Your emotions or opinions are not important or relevant in most cases.

5. Context: always remember that the same email can have a very different effect depending on the context it's sent in. Emails are not separate things outside of real life. As you don't have the benefit of facial expressions and body language, they are very susceptible to the state of mind of the reader. If your reader is in a bad mood, they may interpret your message differently. Be aware of this when you write.

6. Use emails as a way to keep written records of your meetings and important communications with colleagues. This is particularly important in difficult situations or conflicts. Don't fall for the age-old trick of "oh let's talk about it on the phone, or face to face, there's no need to email about this." When there is potential conflict, speak to the person face-to-face or on the phone after you have outlined everything in writing.

7. If an email annoys you, don't reply immediately! Re-read it after your head has cleared up. Try not to introduce your own tone of voice as you read it.

8. Tone of voice is everything! It can make an innocent email sound malicious and vice-versa. Remember this always.

9. Use correct spellings.

10. Unless you know someone relatively well, avoid contractions like we're; use we are in formal writing.

11. Never use 'slang' spellings like 'gonna', even if you know someone well, it looks childish in an email.

12. Use formal English words, such as 'discuss' rather than 'chat', if you're writing a formal document or if you wish to distance yourself from the person.

13. Use correct punctuation: avoid very long sentences unless absolutely needed.

14. Use your own words, or give a clear reference to the source if appropriate.

15. Connect your ideas clearly (e.g. Finally/In conclusion/However)

16. Use correct grammar that makes your meaning clear.

Chapter 1. Business Email: Meetings & Conventions

When you need to send a general email to many people informing them about a meeting or a convention, make sure you keep things short and to the point. Don't give too many non-essential details straight away, as it will clutter the email and make it time-consuming to read.

If you see that many people ask you a particular question after you have sent the initial email, you can compile a FAQ follow-up email to answer the non-essential information or any important information you forgot to include.

Practice Exercise

This is a quick exercise to help you look at an example of a general email sent to a department inviting employees to a conference.

Have a look at the language in the list below and put it in the correct gap in the email. Once you have finished, compare your answers to the example on the next page. After that, you will find a template that you can use in your own communications

will be held /This year/ industry trends /Dear all, do my best to ensure ,
Please find, can do so

.............,

.... the annual Digi-World Conference ....
November 2nd –5th. The conference provides excellent information on
..............., new financial products, and professional development
opportunities. (............ the current agenda attached to this message.)

If you are interested in attending all or part of the program, please
reply to this email directly. I will coordinate our schedule at the
conference and .... that any employee who wants to
participate ...., even if only for a half day.

The conference will be held on the third floor of the RM Hotel, in
the conference centre. Gary Vaynerchuk, Dale Carnegie and Dan
Meredith will organize several car pools.

Regards,

Timothy Ferriss

Answers:

Dear all,

This year, the annual Digi-World Conference will be held November 2nd –5th. The conference provides excellent information on industry trends, new financial products, and professional development opportunities. (Please find the current agenda attached to this message.)

If you are interested in attending all or part of the program, please reply to this email directly. I will coordinate our schedule at the conference and do my best to ensure that any employee who wants to participate can do so, even if only for a half day.

The conference will be held on the third floor of the RM Hotel, in the conference centre. Gary Vaynerchuk, Dale Carnegie and Dan Meredith will organize several car pools.

Regards,

Timothy Ferriss

Sample Fill-in the Blanks Template

Dear all,

This **year/week/month**, the {**Name of conference or event**} will be held {**dates**}. The conference/event provides excellent information on {**Fill with relevant benefits**}. (Please find the **current agenda/schedule/information pack/registration form** attached to this message.)

If you are interested in attending all or part of the program, {**call to action/tell them what they need to do**}. I will {**tell them what you will do**}.

The **conference/event** will be held {**tell them where it will be held**}. {**Tell them about anything else that you or other people are organising in relation to this event**}

Regards,

Your name

Chapter 2. Apologizing in Difficult Times

When you are experiencing difficult times at work, it might sometimes be necessary to admit it and apologize. This will both make you feel better and will provide other people with some context, so that they can better understand your position.

5 Key Phrases for this type of Professional Email:

In this type of email, the following phrases can be useful:

1. "The past several **{days/weeks/months}** certainly have been challenging for all of us"

2. "I understand that **{doing X, Y or Z}** within the time-frame provided simply has not been possible."

3. "I appreciate all your efforts in **{doing X, Y or Z}** when feasible."

4. "Please keep me informed on the progress you are making."

5. "Thank you for your good efforts."

Example Email:

INTEROFFICE MEMORANDUM

TO: [Name]

FROM: [   ]

DATE: [   ]

SUBJECT:

The past several days certainly have been challenging for all of us and I understand that getting the contracts signed within the time-frame provided has not been possible.

I appreciate your efforts in getting them signed when feasible.

Please keep me informed on the progress you are making.

Thank you for your good efforts.

Regards,

James

Professional Email: Late Replies

It can be quite frustrating when someone takes a long time to reply to your email or when they simply forget. If you forget to reply to an email or if you are so busy that it takes you a long time to send an answer, you need to bear in mind that the person on the other end of the exchange has been waiting for you. You should take the time to send a sincere, thoughtful message, acknowledging the fact that your reply is late.

Practice Exercise

This is a quick exercise to help you look at an example of an email reply when it has taken the writer a long time to get back to the other person.

Have a look at the language (1-4) in the list below and put each sentence in the correct gap in the email. Once you have finished, compare your answers to the example on the next page. After that, you will find a template that you can use in your own email communications.

1. I'm sorry that I didn't get back to you sooner about your report

2. I've been frantically busy getting the final contracts in place for the Chapman project.

3. perhaps we can set a meeting to discuss your report for Pat Flynn's new campaign

4. Please let me know if you are available at either of these times

To: [EMPLOYEE]

From: [NAME]

Date: [   ]

Subject: [   ]

Dear Jack,

.... The truth is,

....
....
....

Now that I have a few minutes,

....
....
.... Your ideas certainly sound interesting and I would like to learn more about the market research you have carried out.

I am free this Thursday morning after 10 a.m., and my schedule is also open the morning of the 16th.

....

Regards,

Seth

Answers:

To: [EMPLOYEE]

From: [NAME]

Date: [   ]

Subject: [   ]

Dear Jack,

I'm sorry that I didn't get back to you sooner about your report. The truth is, I've been frantically busy getting the final contracts in place for the Chapman project.

Now that I have a few minutes, perhaps we can set a meeting to discuss your report for Pat Flynn's new campaign. Your ideas certainly sound interesting and I would like to learn more about the market research you have carried out.

I am free this Thursday morning after 10 a.m., and my schedule is also open the morning of the 16th.

Please let me know if you are available at either of these times.

Regards,

Seth

Sample Fill-in the Blanks Template

To: [EMPLOYEE]

From: [NAME]

Date: [   ]

Subject: [   ]

Dear {first name of person the email is directed to},

I'm sorry that I didn't get back to you sooner about **{topic of the person's email}**. The truth is, **{reason why you didn't answer sooner.** *Please note: simply saying "I was busy" with no real reason is worse than not giving any reason. If you don't have a good reason for your late reply, simply apologize and move to the next section}*

Now that I have a few minutes, perhaps we can **{describe what you want to do or arrange}**. Your ideas certainly sound interesting and I would like to learn more about **{mention something you are interested in}**. *(**Note** that this last sentence is optional, but it is a great idea, as it shows interest on your part and the reader will appreciate it.)*

I am free **{provide a rough time and date when you are free to discuss this topic or ask the person to provide you with something. For example, more information on X, Y and Z}**

Regards,

Seth

Chapter 3. Business Emails: How to Give Bad News

"More information is always better than less. When people know the reason things are happening, even if it's bad news, they can adjust their expectations and react accordingly. Keeping people in the dark only serves to stir negative emotions."

Simon Sinek

Giving people bad news is never comfortable or pleasant, but in a professional environment, it can be very dangerous. Try to put yourself in other people's shoes and think how you would like to be treated if you were in their situation.

Try to think about what you know about the people you are going to deliver the news to.

Useful Questions to Ask Yourself Before you Deliver the News:

- What is going on in your audience's professional lives?

- What is going on in your audience's personal lives that you know of?

- Will this affect how they receive the news?

- What objections might they have?

- What fears might they have?

- What suspicions might they have?

- What questions might they ask you?

Sample 1: Communicating a Decrease in Earnings

INTEROFFICE MEMO

TO: [   ]

FROM: [   ]

DATE: [   ]

SUBJECT: [   ]

This has been a particularly challenging year. We have lost a number of strong accounts to competitors and [endured the flooding in our warehouse in March]. As a result of all this, earnings have dropped by 12 %.

Despite being a serious drop in performance, with everyone's help and support, it can definitely be turned around next year. [As you know, we implemented a hiring freeze in October, which we will continue through at least the first quarter. In addition, we have decided we have no choice but to forgo year-end bonuses.]

These steps will enable us to allocate more resources to marketing and customer service, in order to increase the number of new customers. If we attract new customers and retain long-time customer relationships, we will see a rise in earnings in the coming months. [We have already rebuilt the warehouse, adding more space for inspection and shipping, along with a larger loading dock. The rebuilt warehouse can handle 26% more orders per day than the facility we lost.]

Sample 2: Layoffs (Personal Version)

INTEROFFICE MEMO

TO: [   ]

FROM: [   ]

DATE: [   ]

SUBJECT: [   ]

As you all know, our company is currently engaged in a struggle for survival. Lower than expected sales in several of our main product lines have damaged our pursuit of new markets with greater potential. Knowing that customers in [Switzerland and Austria] need our products but that we are unable to reach them is frustrating and discouraging.

Even more discouraging is the knowledge that the only way to fully engage in our fight for survival, is to drastically cut costs as well as reallocate and refocus our limited resources. We simply cannot take every skilled and experienced employee with us on this journey toward a turnaround. As much as we dislike having to give up some of our most valued members of staff, [8 positions], including your position, have been eliminated this week.

We will do everything our limited resources permit to make this layoff more bearable. You will receive [eight months' severance pay in addition to any holiday pay you are entitled to. William Strunk Jr.], assistant HR director, will be available to you for career counseling. He also has a wealth of information on training courses, placement agencies, and other resources.

If our turnaround plans are on target, there may be several openings in [procurement management in nine to twelve months]. I would like to assure you that whenever there are any suitable vacancies, your name will be at the top of our list. We would like to be able to recall all laid-off employees within a year if everything goes as planned.

Sample 3: Layoffs (Less Personal)

INTEROFFICE MEMO

TO: [   ]

FROM: [   ]

DATE: [   ]

SUBJECT: [   ]

The market has changed a lot over the last ten years or so, and our strategy as a business must adapt to these changes. Our main product used to be [TV remotes]. Of course, [TV components have comprised 85] percent of our business for the past [five years now]. At the last board meeting, our directors voted to close our [assembly line] and focus all of our resources on our growing [components production plant].

The [assembly line] will close on [April 12th]. Each of the [22] members of staff will receive a generous severance package, including career counseling, twelve months' salary, and added benefits. Any employees desiring to transfer here to [our growing production plant] will be considered for openings as they occur.

Department heads who expect to have position openings in the next eight to ten months may send job descriptions to the human resources department to match with potential candidates.

Sample 4: Merger

INTEROFFICE MEMORANDUM

TO: [   ]

FROM: [   ]

DATE: [   ]

SUBJECT: [   ]

Blink and the world of financial institutions has changed radically and irrevocably. During the past decade we have witnessed tremendous changes, with insurance companies and other interests increasing their financial services. Competition for customers has grown fierce. To ensure our success and survival, our board has decided to merge this bank corporation with [Statewide Savings Bank].

The merged bank will retain our current [COMPANY] name. The merger will be a pooling of interest, with each of our stockholders receiving [1.62 shares of Statewide common stock] for each share they own in [COMPANY]. The merger is pending regulatory approval and is expected to be finalized in [November].

[Statewide] provides access to additional markets, especially in the North where our market share is small. It also offers the latest in technological and support services, including one of the best data processing centers in the region.

Since we operate in some of the same cities where [Statewide] has branch offices—and in some cases on the same street—[between 11 and 15 branch offices eventually will close]. We do not expect any layoffs due to these closings. Employees will be transferred to other positions that become available.

In fact, the merger will enable us to grow further and faster than either of the two individual corporations could do on their own.

Sample 5: Death

Some people are known for their successes, others for their heart. But few are known for the ability to accomplish great things and their willingness to go out of their way to help others. [*Name of person*] was such a person, and he/she will be sorely missed by the community he/she served.

[*First name*] was never too big to talk to junior members of staff in the office, the ones who needed more than a helping hand. He/she was never too proud to roll up his/her sleeves and help out when there was a problem, no matter how big it was. He/she would always put himself/herself in other people's shoes, no matter how different their opinion may have been.

[*First name*] was truly a special colleague and friend. Losing [*First name*] is a tragedy for those of us whose lives he/she touched, and who were lucky enough to count him among our friends.

Chapter 4. Email Writing: Sales Enquiries & Replies

AREAS COVERED

Sales

Sales Enquiry

Response to Sales Enquiry

Cold e-mail

Business Emails: Sales

According to research carried out by Templafy, it was estimated that the average office worker receives around 90 business emails a day and sends approximately 40 emails a day. This means just one typical company with 1000 employees sends 40 000 e-mails a day!

Organization:

We all know grammar and punctuation are important, but many students forget about other equally important factors such as organization, tone and avoiding clichés and repetition.

Effectively organized writing ensures that important information in the e-mail is clear and that it's easy for the reader to follow and stay engaged. Paragraphs are very important – research has shown that long walls of text often cause people to stop reading.

Linking Words:

Use linking words and discourse markers such as

- Firstly, secondly,

- Subsequently, consequently

- Additionally, moreover

- However,

- In conclusion, to conclude

Punctuation:

One quick note about punctuation – don't be guilty of too many or too few commas!

Exercise 1:

Use appropriate punctuation marks in the following sentences.

1.   We had a great meeting in Wales everyone was very positive about moving forward with the project.

2.   Some employees are more productive in the mornings others do better in the evenings

3.   What are you doing on Monday morning

4.   The CEO is in hospital she has a broken arm

5.   Do you understand why I'm upset

6.   It is a fantastic idea let's hope it works

7.   We will be arriving on Monday morning at least we hope so

8.   A PowerPoint presentation can be a wall between the presenter and the audience.

9.   The Japanese guests sat in the corner most of the night but in the end they joined us and we had a very fruitful meeting.

10. In the words of Gary V life shrinks and expands on the proportion of your willingness to take risks and try new things.

Answers

1. We had a great meeting in Wales - everyone was very positive about moving forward with the project.

2. Some employees are more productive in the mornings; others do better in the evenings.

3. What are you doing on Monday morning?

4. The CEO is in hospital: she has a broken arm.

5. Do you understand why I'm upset?

6. It is a fantastic idea; let's hope it works.

7. We will be arriving on Monday morning: at least, we hope so.

8. A PowerPoint presentation can be a 'wall' between the presenter and the audience.

9. The Japanese guests sat in the corner most of the night, but in the end they joined us and we had a very fruitful meeting.

10. In the words of Gary V: 'Life shrinks and expands on the proportion of your willingness to take risks and try new things'.

Tone:

Tone is also important, so you should normally avoid certain words in business e-mails. For example, always replace "want" with "would like" in business communication and the response from the reader will be more positive. "Want" is a word you should be very careful with, as it can give the impression that you are demanding something without offering the reader a choice. People don't usually like this.

The same is true for "need", rather say "require". It makes the writing sound less desperate, pushy and unrefined.

More recommendations include:

"Can you deliver in 2 weeks?"

Better Alternatives:

Could you deliver in 2 weeks?

Are you able to deliver in 2 weeks?

Would delivery in two weeks be possible?

"Buy"

Better Alternatives:

Purchase

Acquire

Procure

"Very"

<u>Better Alternatives:</u>

Particularly

Highly

Sometimes, as in the case of "very", the word itself is neutral but used rather repetitively so in writing try to ensure that you don't repeat the same words all the time - use appropriate synonyms. The same goes for words which have become clichés such as hard working, motivated and a team player. Use alternatives which stand out from the masses. And lastly, don't even attempt business writing if you aren't completely familiar with the present perfect tense as it is so widely used in formal writing.

"Give me"

<u>Better Alternative:</u>

Provide me with

"Just"

<u>Better Alternative:</u>

Merely

Refer to Addendum A for the complete vocabulary list containing a few more examples.

Sample Template for Sales Enquiry

In many cases the first point of contact between the sales team and potential consumers is the enquiry e-mail. Prompt and professional responses to these enquiries are hugely important in giving the customer a good first impression and this in turn translates into increased sales revenue.

The initial enquiry is usually to request more information, common requests being to ask for lead times or to determine if a product which isn't listed on the company website is available.

A *prospective customer*, or *prospect* for short, is also known as a *lead* (not to be confused with *lead times* as previously mentioned).

The following e-mail is from Jennifer Kovac who works for the Procurement Department of a fictional health food store in New York called Idyllic Earth Health Market. She is reaching out to a few companies to source more products for the company.

Dear Sir or Madam,

My name is Jennifer Kovac and I work for the Procurement Department at a company called Idyllic Earth Health Market. We are a New York-based health food store and we would like to expand our range of medicinal herbs - I'm particularly interested in the cancer bush.

Could you please provide me with a price list of all the products that you supply?

Many thanks

Regards

Jennifer Kovac

Procurement Clerk

Idyllic Earth Health Market

There are several different structures that you can use to respond to this type of enquiry.

One example of a professional e-mail response to the above enquiry will look like the following:

Response to Sales Enquiry

Dear Jennifer,

Many thanks for your enquiry. Yes we have Cancer Bush (Sutherlandia Frutescens) in stock and can deliver to your area at no extra charge. How many would you like to purchase?

We have many more wonderful medicinal plants in stock, even rare Marshmallow (Althea Officinalis) seeds.

I have attached a pricelist of all our products for you.

Please let me know if you require any more assistance.

Kind Regards,

Kristina Longsworth

Sales Executive

Sage Health Foods

Note: You can start the email with *Dear Ms. Kovac* if you wish to be more formal and keep a distance, though this style is used less and less among native English speakers in this type of email nowadays, as it establishes a psychological barrier with the reader. Nevertheless, in some regions, such as Southern Europe and South East Asia, it may be more appropriate to keep it more formal to match the usual email conventions in the local language. Levels of formality also vary between sectors worldwide, so it would be useful to do some extra research into your particular field before deciding.

Sample template for a cold e-mail

A cold email is the digital equivalent of the cold call. These e-mails are more personal and credible than spam but are still unsolicited. However, in some cases they could provide valuable information and even secure appointments. Online surveys show that a large percentage of executives will take an appointment or attend an event after receiving a cold email. You can use this template in any instance where you have never written to someone before and you feel your message will be valuable.

For this type of email to work and for it not be classed as "spam" by the receiver, you must research each prospective client first. Notice how the email contains personalized details that the sales executive has obtained through online and possibly offline research. This is very important, as not only does it show professionalism, but it will also mean you are emailing people who might be interested in your products or services. For example, there is no point in emailing a restaurant chain trying to sell them beauty products!

Dear Sir/Madam,

I represent a medicinal plant and raw materials supplier called Sage Health. Our specialty is organic ingredients, especially hard-to-find ones.

We have rare Marshmallow gel (Althea Officinalis) available for the first time in New York. I thought you might be interested in this product, as it is a highly popular organic anti-aging substance used in beauty creams, and I noticed that your store sells their own range of natural beauty products. I am confident that this product will greatly enhance your offering and increase your long-term revenue.

I am available in your area on Thursday April 18 if you would like to meet and receive some free samples for your store. I could then answer any questions you may have about the product.

Thank you for your time and I look forward to hearing from you.

Kind Regards,

Kristina Longsworth

Sales Executive

Sage Health Foods

Chapter 5. How to be Persuasive

Professionals who want to succeed will need to plan and prepare various forms of written and spoken communication throughout their careers. This may be in the form of an email, a proposal or a presentation where the writer needs to communicate in a persuasive style about an important topic.

Here is an example task:

You are a manager in a marketing company promoting skincare products, and you have to write a proposal for your company to persuade the team to expand into new markets in Asia. In your proposal you need to state:

1. What the current situation is within the company.
2. Any market research conducted or suggestions on what needs to be done in the future.
3. Plans that need to be in place to be successful.

We have used a short proposal as an example here, but these principals can easily be applied to emails and presentations as well.

Before you begin writing, it's important to know your purpose for writing. A proposal requires the writer to persuade the reader.

Always Stick to the Facts.

Give reasons or examples to support your point when trying to convince someone about something. Facts are a great way of persuading people as they speak for themselves. Make use of at least three points.

You can use some transition phrases when you're introducing new points like: *in addition to, however, furthermore, besides that, also, furthermore.*

Facts convince the reader or listener, as they provide solid back-up for what you are saying or going to say. Using factual information to support your opinions is essential, so whenever you prepare a proposal or presentation, make sure you are paying close attention to this, as it can be the difference between winning or losing!

As a part of the introduction, be careful not to include your own opinions but just state "what is".

Using the example, our introduction could look like this:

Introduction

This proposal will provide information about our possible expansion into other markets and a plan of action in order to achieve this successfully.

Be specific and give details.

Avoid using sentences that are too broad or general without specific data to back them up. If you do this, it will make you sound lazy, inefficient and untrustworthy. Once you break your audience's trust, you might as well throw the proposal in the bin, or if you're in a presentation pull your pants downs on stage and start crawling around making chicken noises... Once the trust is gone, it's gone.

Consider this:

Option 1: "People in Asian countries love to buy beauty products and China is the largest country in the region with 1.386 billion people (2017) "

Option 2: "In 2017, the world-wide skin-lightening industry was worth $4.8bn, and it is expected to grow to $8.9bn by the year 2027, spearheaded by an emerging middle class in the Asia-Pacific region. A recent study by the World Health Organization found that 40% of Chinese women regularly use skin-lightening creams."

If you chose option 2, you were right. The second sentence provides more specific concrete words and data. This narrows down the focus and is more likely to convince the audience.

Use the power of three

Giving your reader choices is really effective to convince them. If you provide only one or two points, they will feel like they have limited options. It can feel as if they are backed into a corner with no other options. They may be less likely to agree with your proposal.

Exercise

Decide how persuasive each of the following sentences are and why. Which one is your favorite?

A. Keeping our clients satisfied is of utmost importance.

B. It's important to give whatever our customers need.

C. If attention is not given to the regions, our profits will decrease.

D. There are numerous regions that need market coverage that are within range of our production bases.

E. These regions have high market potential as their infrastructure is growing to meet the market requirements.

F. Many customers have given feedback and suggestions about providing a market base in their area so they need not travel long distance to buy our products.

G. Asian markets don't like the product.

H. Lots of people in Asia love this product, so setting up markets in Asia will be profitable.

Answers to Exercise

Keeping our clients satisfied is of utmost importance.

Comment: This is an opinion and not a fact. It may sound as if it Is the truth, and most people would tend to agree with that. It's still important to stick to things that can be proven. Not the best sentence to use here.

It's important to give whatever our customers need.

Another opinion, which would not be very effective to persuade the reader. It's also arguably quite a dangerous opinion. Does this mean that we give in to any demand, no matter how unreasonable or damaging to the company?

If attention is not given to the regions, our profits will decrease.

This may sound like a fact, but there is no concrete evidence given here. Be careful of using "if" sentences to persuade as it states under, a condition which may not be factual.

There are numerous regions that need market coverage that are within range of our production bases.

This is a good sentence to use in this case as it shows there is information to substantiate the claim. Even though the data may not be explicitly stated, it is something that can be verified and which can lead to further discussion or action.

These regions have high market potential as their infrastructure is growing to meet the market requirements.

This is not too bad, as there is some evidence to support the claim: "infrastructure is growing". It's essential to use opinion supported by some details to make it more persuasive.

Many customers have given feedback and suggestions about providing a market base in their area so they need not travel long distances to buy our products.

A good, persuasive sentence that really will convince shareholders and employers as this is information coming directly from customers. Again, when planning to persuade, it is really important to think of your audience: the reader or the listener. Put yourself in their shoes.

Asian markets don't like the product.

Avoid using sentences like this that are too vague or unclear. This sentence would need more detail to support it.

Where is the proof? We need more information here to be persuasive.

You might change it to: **Studies have shown that Asian markets spend more money on beauty products than on household goods, so introducing beauty creams could prove successful, provided we can execute an effective social media strategy.**

Chapter 6. Professional Emails for Salary Negotiations

This chapter will address the sensitive and important matter of discussing **salaries**, also referred to as **remuneration**. This situation usually arises after an employee has years of employment in a particular role and seeks an increase. Most companies have a set remuneration schedule, which is dependent on the job title and qualifications. However, there are many instances where there are no vacancies for career growth but an employee is making a more significant contribution to the company than when they first started. For example, let's say that a Debtor's Clerk is very successful with getting in revenue for a company especially from unpaid invoices which would otherwise be **written off** as bad debt. Let us also say that this Debtor's Clerk shows strong leadership potential and has recently received another degree or qualification in financial management, software, leadership, regulations or another relevant field. This employee would not be seen in a negative light should they take the bold step of asking for better remuneration, because they have a strong case.

According to an article on TheCut.com, titled *How To Ask For A Raise*, even if your manager says *no* in the end, asking for a raise is very unlikely to damage your relationship, as long as:

A) "You're not asking for an amount that's wildly out of sync with the market for your work"

and

B) "You have a track record of strong work. You aren't likely to fall out of favor simply because you asked to revisit your compensation."

Another piece of advice some may find useful is this, from TheBalanceCareers.com. They suggest having other options as a backup if your manager says *no*, so that you can hopefully walk out with at least a better working environment or another benefit.

Have other options ready to use in the negotiation.

No one wants to hear "no" for an answer, but a rejection can present an opportunity to make another proposition. Do you want to inquire about working from home one day per week? Are you in need of a new mobile phone or laptop for work purposes? Is there a conference or industry event you'd like to attend? Your boss may be more likely to say "yes" to a smaller request after saying "no" to a big one.

The first step in salary negotiations will usually be to secure an appointment with your manager to state your case in person. The benefits to meeting in person are numerous and will definitely help garner a positive response. However, there needs to be a high degree of motivation for the manager to even entertain the idea in the first place and schedule a meeting with you to discuss the matter further, and this is where excellent writing skills are extremely beneficial, a requirement in fact.

How to Write an Email Asking For a Raise:

Do your research on salaries for your position in your area. Firstly, you have to know what your skills and experience are worth in the market. ...

Pick the best time. Does your organization have a policy or habit of granting pay rises during performance review periods for example? ...

Request your pay rise. ...

Back up your request with evidence that you deserve it. ...

Use a call to action. ... (for example, a meeting, a phone call or an email reply)

The following sample e-mail template can be used to start-off the discussion.

Basic Negotiation Dynamics

These five possible results of human interaction, represent the mentality and possible general outcomes of any interaction between human beings. The sixth paradigm "Win", is missing, because a "Win" mentality, when someone doesn't care about the outcome as long they win, inevitably leads to one of the other paradigms.

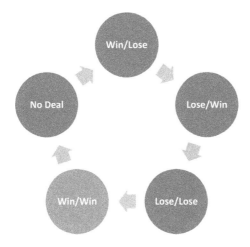

•**Win/Win.** — is a way of thinking, which tries to bring value to other people without accepting injustice. Interactions with other people are not battles but collaborations for mutual benefit and value.

•**Win/Lose.** This is an attitude that tries to establish a situation where you win and the other side loses. While this is necessary in competition and war, it is arguably only beneficial in these particular situations, and not in everyday interactions (business or personal). For example, win-win with employees, colleagues, partners and customers is far more effective and beneficial long term. Win-lose might be appropriate with competitors for example.

• **Lose/Win.** This is what gave "nice guys" a bad reputation. The problem is, real nice guys don´t play this game. This game is more for "scared guys". When someone allows people to do things in order to avoid confrontation, it can cause a lot of damage to everyone involved.

• **Lose/Lose.** This is when two win-lose people, departments or businesses get together. Nobody wins here.

• **No Deal:** the interaction may lead to no agreement or no production of value to any side. This is a No Deal.

What are Win-Win people like?

• They have integrity — they value themselves as a person of consistency and have a specific moral code, which they follow.

• They are mature — they have an understanding of the world, from a "big picture" standpoint

• They have an abundance mentality — there is plenty out there for everyone. We can all benefit from this opportunity!

Professional Email for Salary Negotiation: Template

Dear Mr Johnson,

I have greatly enjoyed working at Trincom Enterprises as a Debtors Clerk. In the years since I joined the company in 2001, I have become a loyal and integral member of the team, and have developed innovative ways to contribute to the department.

For example, in the past year alone, I have achieved the following goals:

• Brought in two new major clients to the company, increasing total sales revenue by 5%

• Voluntarily trained 5 new members of staff, totaling 35 hours of voluntary service

I believe I have gone above and beyond the benchmarks we set for my position in our last yearly appraisal.

I would therefore appreciate the chance to set up a meeting with you to discuss raising my salary by five per cent, which I believe reflects my performance and current competencies, as well as the industry averages.

Once again, I feel very lucky to be a member of this departments and I look forward to taking on my next projects in the near future.

Thank you for your time. I look forward to speaking with you soon.

Sincerely,

Kimberly Jong

Note: With a few changes this template could be used for just about any other salary negotiations.

Salary Negotiation Template 2

Here is a different style of template, which may suit some positions or situations better, if, for example, you cannot think of any clear individual achievements to list in your email, but would still like to request a salary raise.

Dear Mr Johnson,

I have worked loyally and efficiently for Trincom Enterprises as a Debtors Clerk since 2001. I hardly take sick leave, my performance reviews are always positive and my work is always done meticulously and on time.

I would therefore appreciate the opportunity to come and speak to you about a small raise in my salary. I am not asking for a lot, merely 10% on top of what I currently earn.

Please be assured that I understand if my request is denied due to factors beyond the company's control and I will continue working as I always have as I enjoy my work and my team.

Warm Regards,

Kimberly Jong

Chapter 7. Cover Letters & Responding to Job Posts on Linkedin and Email

This section deals with the all-important cover letter, also known as a motivation letter sometimes. The purpose of this letter/email is to highlight your skills, achievements and reasons why you are a strong candidate for the position.

This letter or email absolutely must be tailored to the job posting, it would be a mistake to send the same cover letter to multiple recruiters.

Research as much as you can about the company, after all you should do this anyway. Career choices need to be well-researched in order to be well-informed. Try to make it clear that you have the company's best interests at heart and you don't just want to work for any company, you want to work for that specific company! This is a very important factor, which many job applicants overlook.

Advice regarding resume writing is useful right now because many of the features of resume writing are incorporated into writing a cover letter. For example, hard and soft skills. *Hard skills* are the quantifiable technical skills learnt at educational institutions. *Soft skills* are inherent or developed skills such as emotional intelligence, personality traits and others, which help maximize the execution of hard skills and make an employee easier to integrate into a work environment.

Examples of hard skills:

- Accounting

- Engineering

- Programming

- Technical Writing

- Graphic Design

- Project Management

Soft skills include:

- Good communication and listening skills

- Strong organizational skills

- Self-motivated, hard working

- Patient, friendly, positive

- Emotionally intelligent

Focus

In a cover letter, the focus must be on the company not you. Don't talk and talk about how this opportunity is good for you, focus on how you can help the company. Additionally, don't forget that everyone uses similar words in their cover letters – some words have become so generic these days that you have little hope of achieving your goal of sticking out from all the other applicants when you use them. So never just list a whole bunch of overused words in your cover letter and hope that it does the trick. Find a way to showcase your unique strengths and experiences and how these are the perfect solution to the company's problems.

Cover Letter Example 1

On a sunny Wednesday afternoon a certain Lisa Chan came across her dream job...

Execu Max is a growing recruitment agency focusing on the needs of the IT industry. We are expanding rapidly and are currently in need of a vibrant and experienced Recruitment Manager for our newest office in Cape Town. The new Recruitment Manager will be required to manage a team of 23 recruiters. Preference will be given to well-spoken energetic individuals as the company's social media activities include a corporate vlog.

Ms Chan's winning cover letter:

Lisa Peterson

123 Main Street

Pretoria, SA, 5432

+12 345 6789

lisap@gmail.com

April 1, 20xx

Jacqui van der Merwe

Director, Human Resources

Execu Max

1111 Avenue

Cape Town, SA 6789

+98 765 4321

Dear Mrs vd Merwe,

I'm writing to apply for the position of Recruitment Manager for your head office in Cape Town, as advertised on LinkedIn. I have an MBA in Human Resources and am currently managing the recruitment staff at Talent Scouts. I was promoted from Assistant Recruitment Manager to Recruitment Manager two years ago. Execu Max needs someone who can also contribute to the company vlog and I have experience in that regard. I currently create and edit videos for an organization I founded and am articulate, vibrant and comfortable in front of a camera.

My proudest achievement was about half a year after I first started working at Talent Scouts and initiated a migration to a better ATS (applicant tracking system) which helped the staff increase the amount of applicants on file. It was tough – some of the older staff struggled with the change as they weren't very computer literate and staff morale was very low. But I managed to keep the staff motivated, paired up each senior member with a younger member for a fun "Two Week Challenge" and the end result was increased revenue, skill transference and an all round better working environment.

I feel that Execu Max will benefit greatly from my expertise and enthusiasm and I would very much appreciate the opportunity to work for such a prestigious company. My current employer is more than happy to give me a glowing reference because he is aware that I would love to live closer to my family in Cape Town.

Thank you so much for your time and I will follow up next week with a call.

Regards,

Lisa Peterson

Cover Letter Example 2

This is a great example of a cover letter when you are a recent university or college graduate looking for employment.

Job Advert:

Junior Desktop Support Engineer (MKT176)

Position immediately available for a Junior Desktop Support Engineer to be based on client site in Rosebank.

Ideally you should have your own vehicle, have previous experience in a Microsoft environment, diagnosing and troubleshooting software and hardware issues and installing applications and programs.

In this role you would be responsible for resolving network issues, configuring operating systems and using remote desktop connections to provide immediate support. You need to be comfortable providing support telephonically and via messengers.

To be qualified for this role, you should hold a qualification in a relevant field, like Computer Science, IT or Software Engineering. Microsoft or similar certification is a plus. If you're naturally a helper, enjoy assisting people with computer issues and are able to explain technical details simply, we'd like to meet you.

Ultimately, you will be a person our customers trust. They will rely on you to provide timely and accurate solutions to their technical problems.

- *Research and identify solutions to software and hardware issues*
- *Ask customers targeted questions to quickly understand the root of the problem*
- *Track computer system issues through to resolution, within agreed time limits*

From: https://www.careers24.com/jobs/adverts/1550363-jnr-desktop-support-engineer-mkt176-

Neville Medhora 085 669 2587

28 January 20xx,

Kontak Recruitment

Dear Sir/Madam,

I am an IT graduate from UNISA and I would like to submit my application for the position of Support Engineer as listed online. I specialized in Networking and Security.

Your client is looking for someone who can quickly provide customers with assistance. To me this is one of the most important job duties, as good customer service is vital to retaining and growing revenue. This is something that I know I am very good at, because I not only have the required technical skills to do the job but I also have a lot of patience and a friendly positive nature. I was popular at university for being the go-to guy for computer issues at my halls of residence and even with some of the teachers. My hardware skills are also very good and I am familiar with both Microsoft and Linux.

Please view my attached CV for more details. I have my own vehicle and driver's license.

Thank you for your time and I look forward to hearing from you.

Best Regards,

Neville Medhora

Case Study Analysis

The cover letter above is sincere and concise. The candidate has no work experience but does not focus on this in the letter. Instead, the focus is on his skills and how they will benefit the company. His direct reference to elements of the job advert show that this cover letter is specifically tailored to that company's requirements.

Cover Letter Example 3. Dealing with Potential Objections

The following case study is for Mary Stewart, a single mother of two who was out of the job market for a few years as she wanted to focus on her children. Being a dedicated mother is an admirable trait, but companies unfortunately have to think about who is best for the company's interests. Anyone who has been out of the job market for a few years will very likely be at a disadvantage – their skills could be out of date, the market conditions could have changed, and so on. Also, parents often have emergency child-care issues and may need to take a day or two of leave out of the blue, and companies fear the effects of these issues on productivity. This was rarely an issue in the past, as mothers usually stayed home to take care of their children on a more permanent basis, leaving the men free to focus on work.

Modern problems require modern solutions and parents, especially single parents, need to assure companies that they have a strong support structure in place that will minimize issues. Have a look at how Mary addresses these issues in her cover letter.

We are going to skip the usual basic cover letter content and go straight to the part where she deals with the perceived objections.

"Being a parent is a big responsibility and I wouldn't want my parental obligations to interfere with my duties at work, or vice versa. To that end, I have ensured a strong support network for my family in the form of multiple family members who can assist me, and have also signed up for an account with an emergency babysitting service in the event that my children are unable to attend school and there are no family members able to assist.

I have been out of the market for a little while, however this has had zero impact on my skills, as I feel that as a Personal Assistant the most important thing is exceptional organizational skills, something I have always inherently had. I was most recently the PA to not only one director but three! Tricky at times but I thrived on the pressure.

Kindly see my resume for more details of my career achievements.

Case Study Analysis

Mary is straightforward and professional in her response. We get the sense that she would indeed be an efficient and organized employee – she was an assistant to three busy directors in a company and notice how she organized her childcare, even creating a contingency plan as a backup!

Cover Letter Example 4. The Phoenix Method for Returning to Work after Unemployment

There is one more cover letter which we need to examine – the cover letter for the person who has been unemployed for a long time. We started off with someone who already had a job. These candidates are easy to hire because they have a proven track record and can afford to only apply for jobs that really interest them, so the company feels the employee stands a better chance of being a good fit. The second type was for a recent graduate, fresh and more cost-effective for junior roles. Then came someone who voluntarily left the workforce, so we can assume they left on good terms and weren't dismissed, also a positive.

Onto our fourth scenario – someone who has been out of work for a long time. The usual reason for a long gap in employment is economic factors in the job market – there are simply not enough jobs available in that area or industry because of downsizing. In this case it is easy to explain the absence, and after mentioning your redundancy, if this is what happened, you can add parts from the third example seen just before this one, where we examined a candidate who had been out of work for a while. This will help you to deal with potential objections or doubts that the employer may have.

You want to assure prospective employers that you not only stayed proactive by keeping up to date with the latest industry relevant news and technology or methodology, but you have even improved as an employee, not the other way around. It's all about how you frame your experiences!

Being out of work for a while can be a little personal and painful to talk about. So don't. Focus on what you have been doing to improve and keep up to date with the market.

If you were fired or made redundant for something negative on your part, or something that could be interpreted in that way, then you should try to avoid mentioning it if possible. If it is something on record, which the new employer can and will check, it is probably best to be honest if asked. You can then focus on showing how that experience has helped you improve as an employee and as a person.

Example Case:

Meet Henry. Henry is a 38 year-old recovering alcoholic. He was employed as a Warehouse Manager for 13 years before being dismissed after he was charged with one-too-many drunk driving incidents and had to spend 12 months in prison. Henry felt deeply ashamed of the incident and was determined to get better. He attended AA meetings regularly and did voluntary community service. But his unemployment was getting to him, especially as he couldn't lie because although his previous company wasn't going to mention it to prospective employers, he had a criminal record and was overlooked in favour of more suitable candidates. He was starting to get desperate. His biggest fear was that his unemployment would eventually destroy his resolve and cause him to go "back onto the bottle".

On the next page, you will find a sample of what Henry could write.

Dear Sir/Madam,

I am writing to apply for the position as Inventory Stocker at JC Enterprises.

I have previous experience, as I started from being a stocker and worked my way up to the position of Warehouse Manager at XYZ Ltd between 2001 and 2012. Due to my leadership skills and attitude to work, my staff were motivated and worked hard for the company, not even grumbling about overtime. Because of this, the warehouse performed very well and the customers were happy, so our customer retention rates were never a problem.

Transparency is for me the best policy so I will be upfront about why I am without work – I suffered from alcohol addiction and was I dismissed.

I have successfully overcome my alcohol addiction problems and my experience has really changed me for the better. I've been sober for over 2 years now, and even though my unemployment has made me very stressed, my willpower and support programmes keep me on the right track and I have an active and productive life.

Your company is a very busy one with many customers, so employing me would be a good choice as I would require no training, only to be made familiar with company-specific procedures. I could get straight to work after that.

Additionally, I have retained my subscription to Warehouse Weekly, an online magazine devoted to warehousing and logistics. There are a number of ideas I have on how to maximize efficiency which may be of interest to you.

Any chance of employment at your company would be greatly appreciated and I will follow up next week with a call.

Kind Regards,

Henry Tovey

Case Study Analysis: The Phoenix Effect

Henry's focus is on how he can help the company and this comes through clearly in the first paragraph. In fact, he is almost the perfect employee – except for his past misdemeanours. But he shows humility and growth, which are admirable qualities in both employees and humans.

In classical mythology, the Phoenix was a special bird that lived for five or six hundred years in the Arabian desert. After this time, it burnt itself on a funeral pyre and rose from its own ashes with renewed youth to live through another cycle. The idea of the Phoenix is often used to describe the glorious reinvention of someone or something after a disaster and against all odds. Everybody loves a good old-fashioned comeback, and the recruiter is no different.

The recruiter is human, and human emotions influence decisions. Telling your story in a way that speaks to people's emotions as well as to their logical side is usually a winner. Everyone roots for the fallen hero who rises from the ashes like a Phoenix to take over and be successful. Everybody loves and respects good, relentless people who refuse to give up and keep trying and learning and improving. Don't overdo the personal story, but if you have no choice, then use it to your full advantage, never forgetting that it must be accompanied by logical, sound evidence to convince the recruiter.

In these cases, where the employment gap looms over you, keep it sincere but professional and dignified. Don't beg, and leave out any religious references as this does not directly pertain to the job at hand. However, if it is a religious school or entity that you are applying to, perhaps it wouldn't be remiss to mention that your religious beliefs are the same and that this would make you a good fit for the corporate culture.

Keep the focus of your story on how you can help the organization and not on the hard-ships you have been through. If you frame your story right, you can make your biggest vulnerability into your biggest strength.

You just need to devise a plan and organize your thoughts so you express it in a way that speaks to people.

Addendum A- Vocabulary list

Revenue – income, profit,

Lead times – delivery times

a lead – a prospect or prospective customer

Procurement Department – the part of the company responsible for all the buying

E-mail signature vs signature - An email signature is a block of text appended to the end of an email message which often contains the sender's name and contact information. A signature is a person's name written in a distinctive way as a form of identification in authorizing a cheque or document or concluding a letter.

Recipient – receiver

Remuneration – salary (think Reward)

Meticulously – flawlessly, perfectly, with great attention to detail

Team – in corporate, team usually means your colleagues, particularly those in your department for example the sales team.

Write off – phrasal verb - an elimination of an item from the books of account.

Admin - verb – short for administration. This refers to work which involve handling paperwork, filing, copying and so on. When you empty your deleted files folder, reorganize your files and folders, rename files to make them easier to identify later, file away printed invoices or signed contracts in files or any other activity like this then we say you are doing admin.

Vibrant – lively, having a lot of energy and enthusiasm. Can refer to colours or people.

Incumbent –although rare nowadays it is still used as an alternative word for a potential employee in job postings.

Vlog – the visual/video equivalent of a written blog

Vying – competing for

Inherently - in a permanent, essential, or characteristic way.

Another example is "the work is inherently dangerous". To remember this word in the context we used, think of how we INHERIT assets from our parents. We also inherit genes from them and inherent characteristics are like characteristics that cannot be taught, we are born that way.

Contingency - a future event or circumstance which is possible but cannot be predicted with certainty or a provision for a possible event.

Professional Email Vocabulary: Make your Emails more Professional

The following list has synonyms, which project more professionalism or variety to your business writing.

Need - require

Can you deliver in 2 weeks – – could you/are you able to, would delivery in two weeks be possible

Buy – purchase, procure

Very – particularly

Give me – provide me with

Just - merely

Help - assist

Sell – supply

Chapter 8. Emailing a Reference

In this section, we will examine an essential type of business email: the letter of reference.

Firstly, we will suggest ways you can organize your writing, and then we will look at the kind of language you should be using. Finally, we practice essential language, grammar and vocabulary that will help you gain more credibility when you write.

Emailing a Reference

In this type of business email, you are required to provide a reference for a colleague or friend to a prospective employer or partner.

You may find it helpful to note down useful expressions that you can include,

Some Useful Language for this type of letter or email

I have known X for ....

I am confident that ....

I have no hesitation in recommending him/her ....

X is sociable, reliable, self-confident, outgoing

X possesses a thorough grounding in ...

stand him in good stead

as is shown by the fact that ...

There are four important components: content, organization, language and communicative achievement. Including all the relevant content in your letter and presenting it clearly is vital.

Here is a typical example of a formal email. We will practice identifying key content, working through the task chronologically.

Read the example and answer the following question.

1. What is the first key piece of information you need to refer to in your answer?

A colleague of yours is applying for a job in a popular marketing agency, as an Online Marketing Consultant for English speaking clients. The marketing agency has asked you to provide a character reference for your colleague. The reference should indicate how long you have known each other. It must also include a detailed description of the person's character and the reason why he or she would be suitable for the job.

Write your reference. (220-260 words)

First thoughts

It's important to use a formal register. For example:

"To whom it may concern,

Mary and I have been working together at J&J Marketing for 10 years.

…………..."

2. What is the next important information?

We need to pay attention to the type of job we are writing the reference for. The job in this case is an Online Marketing Consultant for a marketing agency. It is important to remember that the information we provide must be relevant for this position.

3. What qualities or skills does a suitable candidate for almost any job need to have?

You can use the following ideas for any job reference.

i. Personal and social skills (people skills/inter-personal abilities): The successful candidate will need to have good personal and social skills so, if applicable, we must emphasize the person's personal and social skills in the context of their application.

ii. Time-management ability is another skill that every person needs for a job, so regardless of the job you are presented with, you can talk about this.

4. Previous experience.

We need to mention any relevant work the person has done in the past that will support their application. Again, we could link this with the earlier part about their people skills or about their time-management skills.

We need to show the person is suitable for the post, but this doesn't necessarily need to be in a separate paragraph. You can write about their experience in the same paragraph whilst you describe their character and skills.

Alternatively, it could be something you include at the end of the letter but either way, you always need to emphasize the person's suitability for the post.

Organization:

Read the example again and answer the following questions.

1. How many paragraphs would you have?

2. Which paragraphs would deal with which issues?

Example Question

A colleague of yours is applying for a job in a popular marketing agency, as an Online Marketing Consultant for English speaking clients. The marketing agency has asked you to provide a character reference for your colleague. The reference should indicate how long you have known each other. It must also include a detailed description of the person's character and the reason why he or she would be suitable for the job.

Write your reference. (220-260 words)

One idea is to organize this around two or three content paragraphs along with an opening and closing paragraph, so four or five paragraphs in total.

Paragraph 1

The first paragraph is obviously going to deal with our reason for writing. In this case, to write a reference. In a reference email, the first main content paragraph usually outlines the person's skills and experience, perhaps including any relevant qualifications they might have. So in this first paragraph we could answer the sections which are outlined in the example exercise above.

Paragraph 2

Then, we could move on to look at the person's character and personal qualities.

We could deal with the person's suitability for the post in these two paragraphs if we wanted to or we could choose to have a third content paragraph where we emphasize the person's strengths once again.

Finally, we would end the email with a closing statement such as

"Please do not hesitate to contact me if you require any further information".

Writing your email in a logical way like this, especially if you leave a line or a space between each paragraph, will make it coherent overall and will give the reader a visual guide to the organization of your ideas. It will also help you deal with the main sections of the email in a logical order.

Expressing Ideas:

Now we'll look at some of the ways you can link ideas in and between sentences, to express your ideas within paragraphs.

Linking Words:

The first method is the use of straightforward linking words that you've probably used in your writing for a while. Words or expressions like "firstly" or "in addition", or "for instance". These enable you to link ideas quickly and efficiently.

Discourse Markers:

These are slightly more formal linking words or expressions, such as "moreover", "furthermore" or "by way of example".

Exercise 1:

Look at the gaps in the sample answer below:

Where could you use these linking words and discourse markers to complete the text? You will not need to use all of them.

Firstly, in addition, for instance, moreover, furthermore or by way of example.

Sample Answer (Character Reference):

To whom it may concern,

Jane and I worked together at J&J Marketing for 10 years.

It is my pleasure to recommend her for the position of Online Marketing Consultant at XL Consulting.

1....................., Jane is a self-confident and outgoing person, who finds it easy to relate to people from all kinds of backgrounds.

During her time at J&J Marketing, Jane proved to be passionate, communicative, hard-working and excellent at managing her time. 2....................., Jane is the kind of person who works well with others, as she displays great sensitivity and empathy. She was always willing to contribute to the team and help her colleagues. 3................... at J&J

Marketing, she was popular and fully committed to the organization's objectives.

Jane mentioned to me that this role at your company would involve dealing with corporate clients and I believe that she is remarkably well-suited for this task. 4.................... at J&J Marketing, Jane demonstrated excellent communication skills dealing with corporate clients on a daily basis. She also has a keen interest in new media, which I am sure will stand her in good stead when she is helping clients.

I recommend Jane without reservation — she would be an excellent asset to your company.

Please do not hesitate to contact me if you have any questions.

Sincerely,

Your name and Surname

Sample Answer (Letter of Reference/ Character reference):

Now you can check your answers by reading "Sample Answer (Letter of Reference)" below:

To whom it may concern,

Jane and I worked together at J&J Marketing for 10 years.

It is my pleasure to recommend her for the position of Online Marketing Consultant at your XL Consulting.

Firstly, Jane is a self-confident and outgoing person, who finds it easy to relate to people from all kinds of backgrounds.

During her time at J&J Marketing, Jane proved to be passionate, communicative, hard-working and excellent at managing her time. In addition, Jane is the kind of person who works well with others, as she displays great sensitivity and empathy. She was always willing to contribute to the team and help her colleagues. Moreover, (Furthermore) at J&J Marketing she was popular and fully committed to the organization's objectives.

Jane mentioned to me that this role at your company would involve dealing with corporate clients, and I believe that she is remarkably well-suited for this task. By way of example, (For instance) at J&J Marketing, Jane demonstrated excellent communication skills dealing with corporate clients on a daily basis. She also has a keen interest in new media, which I am sure will stand her in good stead when she is helping clients.

I recommend Jane without reservation — she would be an excellent asset to your company.

Please do not hesitate to contact me if you have any questions.

Sincerely,

Your name and Surname

Analysis:

Well done if you answered correctly, but be careful when you write, as there is always the danger that you can overuse expressions like these. If you overuse these expressions, it can make your writing look unnatural and may give the impression to the reader that you don't really understand how to use them. To avoid this problem, let's look at some other cohesive devices you can use to help you organize your ideas.

Reference pronouns:

Reference pronouns like *this, that, they* or *it* are commonly used to refer back to something or someone recently mentioned.

Relative clauses:

Relative clauses can be used to give added information to a statement and they allow you to link ideas together in well-formed sentences.

Substitution:

Other forms of cohesive devices include things like substitution. This is where you use a synonym for example to refer backwards or forwards to a connected point in the text.

E.g. Replacing a verb phrase:

The management team at J & J Marketing were very happy with Jane, and so were the rest of the staff (and the rest of the staff were also very happy with her).

Using paragraphs and a variety of cohesive devices effectively will help you to produce a well-organized piece of writing. When you are reading other people´s writing, make a point of looking out for cohesive devices like the ones we have looked at in this section.

Email Hacks to Get Your Inbox under Control

Most people dread their Inbox every morning. Have you ever felt that dread of opening your inbox because you know you are going to have a tonne of messages or time-consuming tasks? Few people actually have a proper handle on it. Email is a reality we can't efficiently work without in most jobs nowadays, but things don't have to be stressful.

1. Forget Inbox 0. Focus on making your own email communication concise and effective. Simple miscommunication can lead to extra emails being exchanged and as a result, a lot of wasted time on both ends.

2. Establish an email quota where you only spend a set amount of time per day focusing solely on your emails. Forget your non-urgent emails after that and get on with your work. Stop checking your emails constantly and answering less important emails immediately, leave the less important communications until your next email session.

3. While it's essential to establish some basic rules for email, you shouldn't wait several days to deal with them, as the messages will accumulate, and before you know it, you will be buried in emails which need answering today because you left it so long.

4. Use a mass unsubscribe service provider such as Unroll.me to get rid of all of those unwanted email newsletters without having to unsubscribe from each one individually.

Bonus Chapter: The 4 Most Persuasive Words in the English Language

1. "You".

Studies show that using the word "you" gets people interested and engaged.

2. Names

Use people's name. Research also suggests that we trust and engage more with someone if we hear our name being spoke or read it in a message.

3. "Free"

In his book *Predictably Irrational*, Dan Ariely carried our a small study, where he offered participants a choice between a Lindor chocolate for 15¢ and a much cheaper Hershey's Kiss chocolate for 1¢. The Lindor truffle chocolate won even though it was 15 times more expensive. However, in the next stage of this study, he offered the same Lindor chocolate for 14¢ and the Hershey's Kiss free. This time almost 100% of participants chose the Hershey's Kiss chocolate. What lesson can we learn from this study? People will often make different decisions even if the value proposition is basically the same, just because something is free.

4. "Because".

This is an extremely powerful word, even if you don't give a real reason! In his bestselling book *Influence: The Psychology of Persuasion*, Robert Cialdini discusses a study carried out using photocopying machines. In the fist stage of the study, people tried to persuade other people to let them jump the queue at the photocopying machine with the sentence "Excuse me, I have 5 pages, may I use the Xerox machine?" This sentence had a 60% success rate. In the next stage of the experiment, people used the sentence "I have 5 pages, may I use the Xerox machine because I'm in a rush?". Being "in a rush" is definitely not a great reason, but in this stage of the experiment, an amazing 94% of people allowed that person to go in front of them.

Essential Language for Better Writing

PROFESSIONAL ENGLISH WRITING

USEFUL EXPRESSIONS DESCRIBING GRAPHS

- …significantly declined…
- …remained the same..
- …reached a plateau…
- …rose dramatically…
- …fell slightly…
- …fluctuated…
- …increased steadily…
- …fell gradually…
- …decreased steadily…
- …remained stable…
- …recovered…
- …fluctuated dramatically…
- …rocketed…
- …plunged…
- …a dramatic fall…
- …a period of stability…
- …a sight dip…
- …it doubled…
- …it halved…
- …increased sevenfold (7 times)
- …increased fourfold (4 times)
- …proved to be the most popular…
- …began the year higher , however by the end of the year …
- …followed the same sale trend..
- …were consistently the lowest…
- …A similar pattern is also noted on…

- ...With regards to...
- ...is in favour of...
- ...is similar/ dissimilar...

SUMMARY

- ...It can be seen from the data that...
- ...saw barely any increase...
- ...considerably fewer that...
- ...Thereafter... = Afterwards...
- ...stabilized at just ....level
- ...numbers rose but much less significantly...
- ...As regards...
- ...hovering at this level until...
- ...In conclusion...

TALKING ABOUT THE FUTURE

- ...the estimated sales for...

- ...It is anticipated that...

- ...Meanwhile, it is estimated that before increasing to...

- ...As it can be seen

- ...The overall sales trends for... are forecast..

REPORTING

- People *said* it was...

- People *mentioned* that it was...

- People cited that it was...

- People stated that it was...

- People saw it was...

- People regarded it was...

- People claimed that it was...

- People considered it was to be...

- People rated ....as being...

- By contrast , it was cited that...

- The bar chart indicates a survey on ....on factors...

- Whereas... there are contrasting results...

DESCRIBING THE PROCEDURE

- The procedure for… is as follows.
- In order to …the following process takes place.
- First of all…
- Then…
- After that…
- At the next stage…
- This is done by…
- Finally…
- This completes the procedure.

OTHER USEFUL PHRASES TO REPORT

- In all cases there was an increase in...

- By far...

- This figure had more than doubled...

- The second greatest volume of...

- An increase of approximately...

- ...showed significant rises were...

- At the lower end of the scale...

- The chart confirms the increased popularity of...

- The trend was reversed...

- The trend confirmed...

- ... rate was at its highest but then it started to decrease.

OTHER USEFUL PHRASES FOR REPORTS AND PROPOSALS

- If you consider… you could be convinced by an argument in favor of….
- But you have to think about another aspect of the problem…
- I do not feel this is a direct cause of…
- Of course it goes without saying that…
- There has been a growing body of opinion that..
- … the situation can be addressed by adopting the methods mentioned above…
- While I admit that… I would argue that…
- One approach would be…
- A second possibility would be to…
- Obviously,…
- However,
- This suggests that…
- In addition…
- To sum up…
- In fact..
- I tend to disagree…
- I am unconvinced by…
- Overall,…
- In the final analysis…
- Ultimately,…
- To conclude…
- In conclusion…
- On the other hand…
- There is no doubt that…
- This could involve…

- Thirdly…

EXPRESSING VIEWS

- I would argue that…
- I firmly believe that…
- It seems to me that..
- I tend to think that…
- People argue that..
- Some people think that…
- Many people feel that…
- In my experience…
- It is undoubtedly true that..
- It is certainly true that….

REFUTING AN ARGUMENT

- I am unconvinced that…
- I don not believe that..
- It I hard to accept that…
- It is unjustifiable to say that…
- There is little evidence to support that…

PROVIDING SUPPORT

- For example,…
- For instance,…
- Indeed,…
- In fact,…
- Of course,…
- It can be generally observed that…

- Statistics demonstrate…
- If this is/were the case…
- Firstly,…
- Naturally,…
- In my experience…
- Let me illustrate…

DEFINING/EXPLAINING

- I would argue that…
- By this I mean…
- In other words..
- This is to say…
- To be more precise..
- Here I am referring to …

USE SPARINGLY (=a little)

- First/second, etc…
- Moreover..
- In addition…
- Furthermore,…
- Nevertheless/nonetheless…
- On the one/other hand…
- Besides…
- Consequently…
- In contrast…
- In comparison…

USE MODERATELY

- While…
- Meanwhile…
- Although…
- In spite of…/ Despite the fact that…
- Even though…
- As a result…
- However…
- Since…
- Similarly…
- Thus…
- In turn

OTHER USEFUL PHRASES

- My response to this argument depend on what is meant by…
- There is surely a difference between…. and….
- I intend to illustrate how some of these differences are significant to the argument put forward.
- However, whilst I agree that… I am less convinced that…
- I certainly believe that…
- One of the main arguments in favour of…. is that…
- In other words….
- Admittedly, in some ways…
- Surely…
- Arguably..
- Either way…
- In any case…

- The most important point is that…

- Another point is that…

- Of crucial importance , in my opinion, is…

- There is , however, another possible way of defining…

- …that I am in favor of , although I also realize that…

- Therefore…

- There is no doubt that…

- However, it is possible to tackle this serious issue in a number of ways.

- One approach would be..

- …would be particularly beneficial.

- A second possibility would be to…

- …this could involve…

- Many people feel that this is unacceptable because…

- Opponents of… point out that … and argue that…

- On the other hand it cannot be denied that…

- Supporters of…argue that…

INTRODUCING A FALSE ARGUMENT

- It could be argued that…
- Some people would argue that…
- There is also the idea implicit in the statement that…
- It is often suggested that…

DEMOLISHING A FALSE ARGUMENT

- This is partly true, but…
- To a certain limited extant, there is some truth in this…
- However, the implication that… is oversimplification.
- This argument has certain specific logic, but…

PROPOSING A CORRECT ARGUMENT

- It is clear that…
- The real situation…
- Obviously…
- On the contrary…
- It is therefore quite wrong to suggest that…

Free Bonus: 100+ Business Email Templates

Here, you will find a downloadable MS Word booklet with the 100+ Business Email Templates as well as 425 legal documents for business and 25 templates, which you can use or edit as you please.

Sign up for our free resource newsletter, to receive more free resources! ☺

I hope you have found this book useful. Thank you for reading.

https://www.idmadrid.es/vip-resources

IDM Business & Law Academy

Bonus Chapter: FREE BOOK! The Productivity Cheat Sheet

Download your free copy of The Productivity Cheat Sheet: 15 Secrets of Productivity here!

https://www.idmadrid.es/vip-resources

9 781099 134944